STANLEY GIBBONS STAMP COLLECTING SERIES

STAMP COLLECTING

COLLECTING BY THEME

COMPILED BY
JAMES WATSON

STANLEY GIBBONS PUBLICATIONS LTD LONDON AND RINGWOOD

Published by **Stanley Gibbons Publications Ltd**
Editorial, Sales Offices and Distribution Centre :
5 Parkside, Christchurch Road, Ringwood,
Hants BH24 3SH

© *Stanley Gibbons Publications Ltd 1990*

First Published 1983
Reprinted with amendments 1990

Also in this series :

Stamp Collecting—**How to Start**
Stamp Collecting—**How to Identify Stamps**
Stamp Collecting—**How to Arrange and Write-Up a Stamp Collection**
Stamp Collecting—**Philatelic Terms Illustrated**
The Stanley Gibbons Guide to Stamp Collecting

The Author : the late James Watson joined the staff of Stanley Gibbons in 1946 and worked in the New Issues Dept. before becoming a feature writer for Gibbons Stamp Monthly. *He retired from Gibbons in 1981. Mr. Watson wrote several books on philately—most notably the* Stanley Gibbons Book of Stamps and Stamp Collecting. *He also wrote about cine photography and was an expert on picture postcards of the early 20th century.*

Designed by Julia Lilauwala

Printed in Great Britain by BAS Printers Limited, Over Wallop, Hampshire

ISBN 0-85259-043-1

S.G. Item No. 2762

CONTENTS

INTRODUCTION

Every postage stamp has a design, and virtually all stamp designs picture people, places, objects or events. It is the subject of the design and its connotations which attract collectors—and even experienced philatelists—to the picture gallery of stamps or the well-documented story. Collecting stamps by design or theme is not a new idea. Stanley Gibbons sold packets of stamps bearing portraits of Queen Victoria, coats of arms, etc. in his early days, and later made up packets of animals when the Canadian beaver, the kangaroo of New South Wales and the crocodile of North Borneo were novelties. Fred J. Melville, famous philatelist and writer, displayed a 'Postage Stamp Zoo' in his *Boys' Own Guide to Stamp Collecting*, published in 1926.

1–2

In its simplest form the thematic collection is merely an accumulation of stamps depicting animals, birds, butterflies, flowers, churches, railways, ships or whatever subject takes the fancy of the collector. Arranged in orderly fashion within the album, the 'accumulation' becomes a collection reflecting the owner's personal taste and aptitude for display. You are absolutely free to choose the subject and arrange the stamps to your own ideas for your own pleasure and that of your family and friends. Another form of 'thematics' is the narrative or story in which stamps illustrate the progressive development of a theme—it could be the life and career of a celebrity, a famous musician, perhaps, or a well-known painter. Something more ambitious would be 'The Story of Flight', 'The History of the Motor Car' or a telecom saga, 'From Morse to Telex'. This type of collection must be thoroughly pre-planned and researched to provide the necessary 'running commentary' in the album, especially if it is intended for competition.

2–7

8 The life and career of famous people traced through stamps—Prince Charles as a baby with his mother (1950) to his marriage in 1981. The British 1/- stamp shows him at the time of his investiture as Prince of Wales (1969). Musician Beethoven and painter Manet together with stamps depicting their work. The French painting stamps can also be found on 'maximum cards'—popular with many thematic collectors.

9 Some early cars shown on Swedish stamps and old and modern cars on 1982 British stamps.

10 International Education Year (1970).

'Purpose of Issue' defines a third method of thematic collecting which embraces all the stamps issued for an event or institution of national or world significance, regardless of what appears on the stamp. An example was International Education Year (1970) whose scope ranged over a wide variety of design subjects. Whichever subject and style of collecting is adopted, the ultimate joy is finding the stamps after tracking them down in the stamp catalogue.

THEMATIC ORIGINS

As stamps gradually became more and more pictorial—especially as printing methods improved so that many commemoratives and 'picture' stamps of the 1920s and 1930s were miniature works of art in themselves—so more people began collecting them for their designs alone. Generally the stamps were mounted 'as they came' in blank loose-leaf albums with scant attention paid to differences of the species of birds and plants, of the classes of dogs or horses, and mixing ocean liners with warships and so on. It was this haphazard method of collecting and arranging the stamps which roused the opposition and wrath of serious philatelists, and led to the numerous controversies which raged when thematic displays were submitted as entries in national and international competitions, hitherto the preserve of more erudite philatelic studies.

Fortunately, philately's governing body, the Fédération Internationale de Philatélie (F.I.P.), stepped in and drew up a set of regulations for 'Thematic, Purpose of Issue and Subject Collections' in 1967. In the United States, where thematics are known as 'topicals' (from 'topic' or theme), the American Topical Association, founded by Jerry Husak and other enthusiasts in 1949, also published its own set of rules for the guidance of its members. Under these directives the simple subject collection and the similar 'purpose of issue' idea were given little more than authoritative approval, but for the theme or thematic collection it was required that the stamps and supporting material (*i.e.* appropriate photographs, postcard pictures, postmarks, maps, etc.) should be strictly relevant to the story, that it should be titled and adequately introduced, and that the arrangement of the stamps and material should follow a preconceived plan.

The thematic collection is now an established part of the competition scene in national and international events. Of the 45 entries in the Thematic Class of the 'London 1980' International Stamp Exhibition competition at Earls Court in May 1980, there were 42 medal awards, including 10 vermeil and 21 silver medals. This event marked the 'coming of age' of thematic collecting and signalled a decisive victory for the collectors, establishing thematics as an adult and serious form of stamp collecting.

The thematic collection has acquired a new significance and has become something more than the mere accumulation of stamp pictures of anything from aircraft to zebras. During the past 50 years or so it has gradually won respect and recognition by the British Post Office, the Crown Agents and postal administrations all over the world. Strong support for 'picture' collecting has come from the stamp trade, some of whom now specialise in thematics. The old problem of collectors wanting to buy a single stamp from a set of mixed designs seems to have been overcome where conditions of supply permit the purchase of odd values, or single stamps can be purchased from the post office. When the British Post Office issued a set of 'Maritime Heritage' stamps (June 1982), stocks of the 24p Lord Nelson stamp became rapidly depleted at most post offices — indicating a strong thematic interest in Britain's most celebrated sailor.

11 Britain's most eminent sailor— Horatio Nelson (1758–1805) with his flagship H.M.S. *Victory.*

Other thematic developments over the years relate to the collector's choice of subject or theme. While the junior collector or beginner may be content to collect 'animals' or 'birds', the more discerning collector tends to concentrate on one aspect or species of the main subject or theme of which he or she has a specialized knowledge through occupation or hobby. The cat-lover will settle for domestic cats—the short-haired black-and-whites, gingers, tabbies, tortoiseshells and Siamese, or the long-haired chinchillas and Persians—or the 'big cats' of wildlife—the cheetahs, jaguars, leopards, lions, panthers and tigers of Africa, America and India. The thousands of colourful birds on stamps necessitate drastic specialisation—one or more of the 27 orders (comprising 155 families), the song birds or birds of prey, or birds of the geographical zones of the world.

Each year brings its crop of new issues, not only from Great Britain, the Channel Islands, the Isle of Man and the Commonwealth, but also from all the countries of the world, those which we describe as 'foreign'. The average release of about 6000 new stamps each year provides a vast choice for the thematic collector—exciting additions to existing collections or prospective ideas for a completely new and perhaps unusual theme. There are now literally hundreds of different subjects to choose from: you may find one that interests you in the 'ABC of Subjects and Themes' at the back of this Guide.

CHOOSING A THEME

A. The Picture Gallery

12 Great Horntail

The measure of a successful thematic collection is the degree of pleasure and satisfaction you derive from it, and the recipe for success is making the right choice and having the knowledge—both of stamps and your subject—to maintain your enthusiasm and interest. It may be that you already collect stamps and have a subject in mind for a sideline collection—you may even have put some picture stamps aside for that very purpose. If, however, you have no knowledge of the collecting hobby, you are recommended to read a companion in this series called *Stamp Collecting—How to Start* by the same author. You will learn how to obtain stamps and how to handle them, and you will be introduced to the Stanley Gibbons stamp catalogues. The 'Stamps of the World' Catalogue published annually in three parts are very useful for the thematic collector. Stanley Gibbons also publish a range of thematic catalogues, titles available are: Birds, Mammals, Railways and Ships, while *Gibbons Stamp Monthly* magazine will keep you up to date with new issues of stamps.

Most subjects lend themselves to sub-division which should be the basis of the arrangement of the stamps in the album—the actual layout is described in the chapter on 'Albums and Writing-up'. This is best explained by example, for instance the science of entomology, insects, which comprise four-fifths of the animal kingdom and form the *Phylum insecta*, one of the main divisions or *phyla* of that kingdom. This includes all the orders, superfamilies and families of the insect world, from the Odonata (dragonflies) to the Diptera (mosquitoes and gnats, etc.). Ideally the stamps should be arranged to correspond with the scientific register, recording the English and Latin names as captions, but in practice it is probably more straightforward to head your album pages simply as 'Locusts and Grasshoppers', 'Beetles', 'Butterflies and Moths', etc. while having regard to the different families in each group.

If you should decide that butterflies and moths are more colourful and attractive than wasps and bees, and want to create a picture gallery of them alone, no one will blame you. The choice is yours for the making. Classification will be simpler also. The Lepidoptera order includes several large families—the Papilionidae or swallowtails, the Pieridae—cabbage whites, orange-tips, clouded yellows, etc., the Nymphalidae—peacocks, tortoiseshells, red admirals and emperors, and the Lycaenidae—blues and coppers. Butterflies are distinguished by their club-tipped antennae and vertically folded wings, and there are many exotic tropical species on stamps. Moths have pointed antennae and lay their wings flat across their bodies—the principal families are the Saturniidae or giant silkworm moths, the Sphingiidae, including the Death's Head hawk moth, and the Arctiidae or tiger moths. Butterflies and moths are usually identified on the stamps, though not always accurately, and their names can be confirmed in any good reference book on the subject. Collect the unused stamps and group them together in families.

13 Butterflies—Chequered skipper and *Morpho aega.*

Something quite different now, a subject which would appeal to the collector who is a civil engineer—Bridges. It is a picturesque subject and there are some very famous bridges on stamps, among them our own Tower Bridge (the bascule type) across the Thames in London, the Sydney Harbour (single-span arch) Bridge, the Forth (Railway) Bridge in Scotland and the Quebec Bridge in Canada, which are both cantilever bridges, and some famous suspension bridges including the Forth (Road) Bridge, the Verrazano Narrows and Golden Gate Bridges in the U.S.A. The stamps could be grouped in construction styles, by country or even by continent with no need for a continuing story—just notes about each type and captions to the stamps.

14 Major European bridges.

A 'picture gallery' implies a collection of paintings—portraits and landscapes—which is one of the most popular thematic subjects. Every artist of repute is represented on stamps and one can specialise in the works of Rembrandt, the impressionist paintings of Monet and Renoir, the Renaissance classics of the Italian School—Botticelli, Michelangelo, Raphael and Titian, or the robust ladies painted by Goya and Rubens. Again no story-line is necessary—just a self-portrait (if you can find one) of your chosen artist, a few biographical notes and your own gallery of his work on stamps. Here you could judiciously supplement the stamps with picture postcards reproducing one or two paintings which would serve as detailed enlargements of the stamp pictures.

15 Paintings—classical and modern reproduced in miniature on postage stamps.

Music is another entertaining subject for your 'sympathematic' consideration, whether it's your hobby or your profession. Any one of its numerous sub-divisions—composers, orchestras, instruments and players, conductors, opera and ballet, song and dance or features on the symphony, the piano or the violin—can be supported by a wide range of attractive stamps. The symphony first rose into importance with Haydn and was devleoped by Mozart (who wrote 41 symphonies), Beethoven (who somewhat modified it) and Schubert, followed by Tchaikovsky and Brahms. Bruckner's tremendous 'Ninth Symphony' (unfinished) was characteristically dedicated to God, while Mahler, his pupil, composed ten symphonies (again, the last unfinished). Haydn, incidentally, had a proflific output—more than a hundred symphonies and numerous other orchestral works. His pupil, Beethoven, was a child prodigy as a conductor and pianist, and wrote nine symphonies including the famous 'Fifth'.

16 Musical instruments, musicians and scores.

17 Sports of all kinds.

Every kind of sport is depicted on stamps and personal preference, or maybe participation, will prompt your choice of subject. There are fewer stamps for cricket and golf than there are for soccer, tennis and winter sports, but do not be deterred by the difficulty of finding appropriate stamps: picture postcards and commemorative postmarks contribute to a varied and interesting display. The World Football Cup events have provided literally hundreds of stamps from which to choose, while the Olympic Games, held every four years, always bring a crop of new issues covering athletics and all the other Olympic events. For the Montreal Games in 1976, Canada, the host country, issued 35 stamps in 12 sets as well as stamps for the Winter Olympics at Innsbruck and the Olympiad for the Physically Disabled.

The miscellany of designs belonging to a 'purpose of issue' subject—such as the Centenary of the Universal Postal Union (1974)—can be arranged by country, philatelic style, or in groups according to the design motif. These range from portraits of the founder, Heinrich von Stephan, to the well-known U.P.U. monument at Berne, the various forms of mail transport, postmen and symbolic letters and globes. Where a design is uniform throughout a set, only one stamp need be shown, perhaps with ('Set of six')—or whatever—in brackets within the caption. When collecting for your own enjoyment there are no hard and fast rules!

  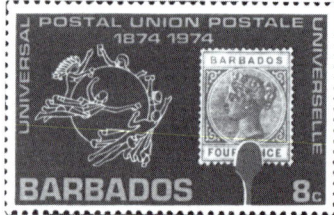

18 Centenary of the Universal Postal Union. Most stamps featured a representation of the U.P.U. monument in Berne. A special postal slogan was used on mail posted in Geneva.

If you want to start a subject collection in a small way (with a modest outlay) then why not *Collect British Stamps?* That is the name of a handy little checklist published by Stanley Gibbons which illustrates all British stamps in colour—it is updated every year, and it will provide a whole host of thematic ideas and possibilities. Hundreds of G.B. commemorative and pictorial stamps with interesting designs have been issued in the past 40 years, and the subjects include Animals and birds; Architecture—castles and cathedrals; Aviation—including Concorde and the R.A.F.; Exploration and discovery; the Christmas Story; Famous people; Flowers and trees; Butterflies; Historical events; Horses and horse-racing; Invention and technology; Literature and Music; Paintings and painters; the Postal services—including Sir Rowland Hill; Railways and ships; Royal occasions; Sport and pastimes; Telecommunications and broadcasting. Subjects which at first glance appear to have limited scope may, to the imaginative and versatile collector, prove to be expansible, not only with unexpectedly related subjects, but with stamps from other countries.

19 Architecture: Four Royal residences shown on stamps issued in 1978. The stamps were printed in miniature sheet format (as shown) as well as in normal sheets of 100. Aviation: one of three British stamps commemorating the first flight of Concorde (1969). Literature: one of four stamps featuring characters from Dickens (1970). Telecommunications: British stamp for inauguration of Pacific telephone cable, COMPAC (1963).

If you decided to feature 'London—Capital City' on G.B. stamps, your list, (taken from *Collect British Stamps*) would be as follows:

1961 *Seventh Commonwealth Parliamentary Conference.*
629 6d. Hammer beam roof, Westminster Hall
630 1s. 3d. Palace of Westminster

20 London buildings from Westminster Hall (1097) to the Post Office Tower (1965)

1964 *20th International Geographical Congress, London.*
651 2½d. Flats near Richmond Park

1965 *700th Anniversary of Simon de Montfort's Parliament.*
664 2s. 6d. Parliament Buildings (Hollar, 1647)

1965 *25th Anniversary of Battle of Britain.*
678 1s. 3d. Air-battle over St. Paul's Cathedral

1965 *Opening of Post Office Tower.*
679 3d. Tower and Georgian buildings
680 1s. 3d. Tower and Nash terrace, Regent's Park

1966 *900th Anniversary of Westminster Abbey.*
687 3d. Westminster Abbey
688 2s. 6d. Fan vaulting, Henry VII Chapel

1968 *British Bridges.*
766 1s. 9d. M4 elevated motorway and viaduct, Chiswick

1969 *British Architecture—Cathedrals.*
800 9d. St. Paul's Cathedral

1973 *400th Birth Anniversary of Inigo Jones.*
936 3p St. Paul's Church, Covent Garden

1973 *19th Commonwealth Parliamentary Conference.*
939 8p Palace of Westminster (from Whitehall)
940 10p Palace of Westminster (from Millbank)

1975 *European Architectural Heritage Year.*
977 8p Royal Observatory, Greenwich
979 12p National Theatre

1975 *62nd Inter-Parliamentary Union Conference.*
988 12p Palace of Westminster (aerial view)

1978 *British Architecture—Historic Buildings.*
1054 9p Tower of London
1057 13p Hampton Court Palace

1980 *'London 1980' International Stamp Exhibition.*
1118 50p Montage of London buildings

1980 *London Landmarks.*
1120 10½p Buckingham Palace
1121 12p The Albert Memorial
1122 13½p Royal Opera House
1123 15p Hampton Court (Palace)
1124 17½p Kensington Palace

Other subjects can be handled in similar fashion, beginning with a list of the stamps you need. Look out for stamps which can be linked to those you have already noted—for example, the ballerina and the opera singer ('British Theatre', April 1982) could be joined with the Royal Opera House stamp while the scene from 'Hamlet' in the same series could be associated with the

National Theatre stamp. Literature and the arts as depicted on British stamps often have links which may be revealed by a close study of the stamp designs and background events.

B. Telling Tales—the Narrative

Starting a narrative or 'story-book' theme requires considerable thought, lots of planning 'in the rough' and possibly some quite laborious research. Your choice of theme should be capable of logical development—and like all good stories it should have a definite beginning, middle and ending. It could be the life story of a famous person (like Sir Winston Churchill), the progress of one of the many branches of medicine or of chemistry and physics from the theories of Robert Boyle to the exciting researches of Albert Einstein, or the history of one of the major industries such as coal and coal-mining, or iron and steel. The oil industry—from early discoveries to North Sea oil with its drilling platforms and rigs—would make a topical subject. Products which affect all our lives, such as coffee, tea, sugar or rubber, would find support from hundreds of stamps.

21 Ballet and Opera and London's Royal Opera House. Shakespeare play and the new National Theatre.

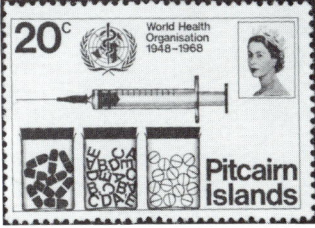

22 Medicine on stamps—drugs, drug abuse and a famous surgeon.

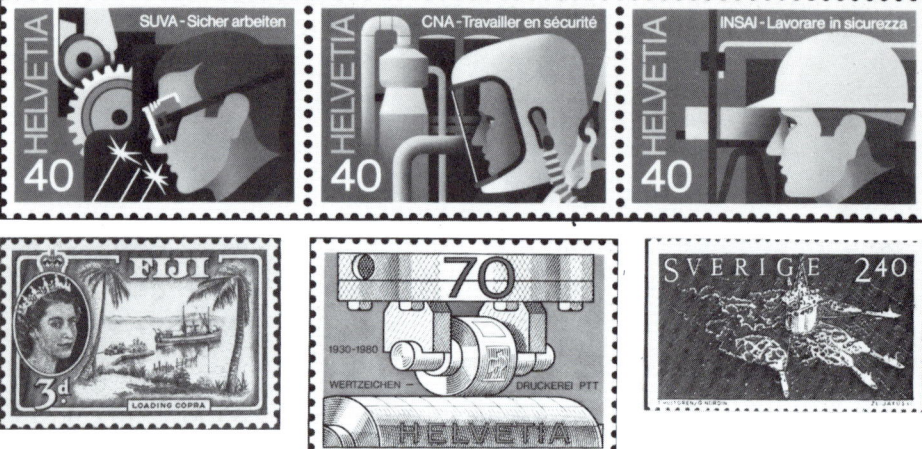

22A Industry & Commerce—from loading copra in Fiji to North Sea oil exploration.

We can learn from others and here is a selection—not to be slavishly copied—of the award-winning entries in the thematic competition class of 'London 1980':

Medical Ecology in Philately. The diseases of man from ancient times to the present day.
Motor Vehicles. Their evolution, traffic, motor racing, etc.
Railways. Their worldwide development
History of Aviation. Balloons, zeppelins, aeroplanes, etc.

23 Aviation and the Telephone—blessings to business but endangering the environment.

The Rotary Presses. The history of writing, typewriting and printing
The Telephone. Its history, technology and place in everyday life
Christopher Columbus. His life and voyages
James Cook: Pacific Pathfinder. His three voyages of discovery
Napoleon: Emperor of the West. Birth in Corsica; the French Revolution; his battles and exile following defeat at Waterloo

The adventures and exploits of the early explorers, navigators and sailors are picturesque themes, but one has to be selective. While the Columbus story can be represented by comparatively few stamps from the sets issued by Spain (1930), San Marino (1952) or the United States (1893), the life and voyages of Captain Cook have received 'saturation' coverage on stamps from Australia, the Cook Islands, New Zealand, Norfolk Island and a dozen other countries, including duplication of portraits, etc. I repeat — be selective!

24 Captain James Cook (1728–79)— explorer *extraordinaire.*

Having chosen your theme — and having assured yourself by a preliminary browse through the catalogue that there are sufficient stamps (but not too many!) suitable for your special collection — your first step is to make a list of the stamps, working through the catalogue country by country noting the relevant details — events, dates of issue, face values and designs and, for easy reference, the catalogue numbers of the stamps. In short, compile your own catalogue, preferably in a notebook, which will become your original source of reference when you come to arrange your stamps in the album. Important to your story is the date or period of the events commemorated on the stamps because your narrative will be arranged according to the time sequence, *i.e.* chronological order rather than the order of your list.

25 Some thematic collectors like stamps used on piece or cover with relevant postmarks. These give added interest.

Every catalogue page must be carefully and closely scanned: don't just look at the illustrations — to economise in space usually only one stamp in a set is reproduced, which means that you must also read the descriptive captions for each listed stamp. However you can skip countries which you know are unlikely to have issued the stamps you are looking for — you wouldn't expect to find stamps relating to polar exploration among the African states, for example. Working through the catalogue is a long and arduous task, nevertheless a most enjoyable one, especially when you find designs which fit precisely into your 'master' plan and contribute, rather like the pieces of a jigsaw puzzle, to your story. Patience is required!

Your personal catalogue has three main functions. First it is a permanent record of the stamps you need: from it you can compile a second, less elaborate, list of the stamps in their chronological order of events—that will be the basis of your narrative, a kind of film-maker's 'storyboard'. Thirdly your catalogue provides yet another list, a 'want-list' of the stamps you will be seeking to purchase. If you are contemplating sending details to a dealer it is essential to quote Gibbons catalogue numbers under each country and which catalogue and which edition you are using. Always state if you want unused or postally used stamps. Unused stamps are preferable as the postmark on a used stamp may obliterate part of the design which should obviously be crisp and clear. However, a commemorative or thematic postmark is acceptable.

The Mutiny on the 'Bounty'

One of the most exciting maritime adventure stories illustrated by stamps is that of the mutiny on the *Bounty* in 1789, when the skipper, Lieutenant William Bligh, and some of his crew were cast adrift in an open boat and survived a marathon voyage. The sequel to these events was the eventual settlement of the Pitcairn Islands and the violent deaths of virtually all the mutineers. Indeed there are two stories here—the life and career of 'Breadfruit Bligh' (as he was known in the Royal Navy), and the exploits of the *Bounty* mutineers. Here is a catalogue list of all the relevant stamps so far issued. The catalogue numbers are quoted.

AITUTAKI (COOK ISLANDS)

1974   *William Bligh's Discovery of Aitutaki.*
114   1c. Bligh and *Bounty*
115   1c. *Bounty*
116   5c. Bligh, and *Bounty* at Aitutaki
117*   5c. Aitutaki chart of 1856
118*   8c. Captain Cook and *Resolution*

26 The Mutiny on the 'Bounty'—some of the many stamps from Aitutaki, Fiji, French Polynesia, Norfolk Island, Pitcairn Islands and Solomon Islands.

119*   8c. Map of Aitutaki and inset location map
* =optional. (Bligh served under Capt. Cook on his second voyage of discovery).
1977   Silver Jubilee.
255   25c. Capt. Bligh, George III and HMS *Bounty*

FIJI

1967   150th Death Anniversary of Admiral Bligh, 'Principal Discoverer of Fiji'.
364   4d. Bligh (bust), HMS *Providence* and chart
365   1s. '*Bounty's* longboat being chased in Fiji waters' (map)
366   2s. 6d. Bligh's tomb (St Mary's Churchyard, Lambeth)
1970   Explorers and Discoverers.
426   8c. Captain Bligh and longboat

FRENCH POLYNESIA

1958   Definitives.
14*   50f. 'The Women of Tahiti' (Gauguin)
* =optional.
1968   Bicentenary of Discovery of Tahiti.
81   40f. Ship's stern and canoe ('Wallis, 1767'.)
(Tahiti was Bligh's original destination, and the mutineers took
Tahiti women to Pitcairn).

NORFOLK ISLAND

1956   Centenary of Landing of Pitcairn Islanders on Norfolk Island.
19, 20 3d., 2s. Norfolk Island seal and Pitcairners landing
1967   Christmas.
92   5c. John Adams' prayer and candle

PITCAIRN ISLANDS

1940   Definitives.
2   1d.   Christian on *Bounty* and Pitcairn Island
3   1½d. John Adams and his house
4   2d.   Lt. Bligh and *Bounty*
5   3d.   Map of Pacific showing location of Pitcairn

5a 4d.   *Bounty* Bible
6 6d.   HM Armed Vessel *Bounty*
7 1s.   Fletcher Christian and Pitcairn
8 2s. 6d. Christian on *Bounty* and Pitcairn coast

1957 Definitives.
19 1d.   Map of Pitcairn Island
20 2d.   John Adams and *Bounty* Bible
22 3d.   Bounty Bay

1961 Centenary of Return of Pitcairn Islanders from Norfolk Island.
29 3d.   Pitcairn Island and Simon Young
30 6d.   Norfolk Island and Pitcairn Islands
31 1s.   Migrant schooner, *Mary Ann*

1964 Definitives.
37 1d.   The *Bounty*

1967 Bicentenary of Discovery of Pitcairn Islands.
67 1s.   Carteret and HMS *Swallow*, 1767

1967   *150th Death Anniversary of Admiral Bligh.*
82   1c. Bligh and *Bounty's* longboat
83   8c. Bligh and followers cast adrift
84   20c. Bligh's tomb

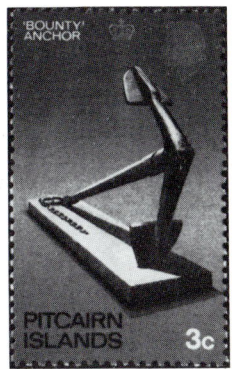

1969   *Definitives.*
94   1c. Pitcairn Island
95   2c. Capt. Bligh and *Bounty's* chronometer
96   3c. *Bounty's* anchor
97   4c. *Bounty* plans and scale drawing
98   5c. Breadfruit pots and plant
99   6c. Bounty Bay
100*   8c. Pitcairn longboat
102*   15c. Fletcher Christian's Cave
103*   20c. Thursday October Christian's house
106   40c. *Bounty* Bible

1976   *Bicentenary of American Revolution.*
167   5c. Fletcher Christian
168   10c. HMS *Bounty*

1978 'Bounty Day'.
185/7* 6c., 20c., 30c. Building, sailing and burning *Bounty* model

1979   150th Death Anniversary of John Adams.
194   35c. John Adams and diary extract
195   70c. Grave and diary extract
* = optional

SOLOMON ISLANDS

1956   Definitives.
91   1s.   Voyage of HMS *Swallow*, 1767 (chart and ship)

1972   Ships and Navigators.
217   15c. Philip Carteret and HMS *Swallow*

TONGA

1953   Definitives.
110*   1s.   Map of Tonga islands
112   5s.   Mutiny of the *Bounty*—Tofua and Kao (*Bounty* and longboat)

From the above list it is apparent that there are approximately 60 stamps representing the dual theme, about half that number supporting the story of William Bligh and the remainder the perhaps predictable fate of the mutineers. Here are the two separate narratives which will enable the reader to select the most suitable stamps.

Bligh of the 'Bounty'

William Bligh was born in Plymouth, Devon, *c.* 1753. He joined the Royal Navy and sailed under Captain Cook on his second voyage of discovery aboard the *Resolution* in 1772–75, exploring Antarctica and visiting Tahiti and other island groups in the Pacific. In 1787 Lieutenant William Bligh, R.N., sailed from Portsmouth in command of H.M. Armed Vessel *Bounty*, ex-*Bethia*, 200 tons, bound for Tahiti on a mission to collect breadfruit plants for transplantation in the West Indies. The easy life on Tahiti completely demoralised Bligh's men and on the return voyage his harsh discipline antagonised his second-in-command, Acting-Lieutenant Fletcher Christian, and others of the crew—on 28 April 1789, while in the vicinity of the volcanic island of Tofua and neighbouring Kao in the Tongan group, they mutinied. Bligh and 18 loyal members of his crew were cast adrift in an open boat, while the mutineers returned to Tahiti, and ultimately settled on Pitcairn Island.

Bligh navigated his longboat westward, through the Fiji Islands (which he recorded in detail) and on past the northern tip of Queensland, eventually landing on Timor in the East Indies after a voyage of some 3600 miles and almost incredible hardship. Bligh was given another command—HMS *Providence*—and once again sailed to the Pacific to collect breadfruit plants, discovering Aitutaki, northernmost of the Cook Islands, and again visiting Fiji, in 1792. He took part in the Battle of Camperdown off the Dutch coast where Admiral Duncan defeated the Dutch fleet in 1797, and in the same year he was present at the infamous mutiny at the Nore. In 1801 he was with Nelson at Copenhagen when the Danish fleet was completely routed, and in 1805 he was appointed Governor of New South Wales. Again he was faced with mutiny and, in 1808, he was imprisoned for two years by the rebels, but in 1811 the ringleader was tried in England and cashiered. Bligh was promoted to Rear-Admiral of the Blue, a rank which he held for six years until his death in London in 1817. His tomb is in St Mary's Churchyard, adjoining Lambeth Palace, in London.

The 'Bounty' Mutineers

The mutiny on the *Bounty* took place in Tongan waters when the ship, commanded by Lieutenant William Bligh, R.N., was returning from a voyage to Tahiti to collect breadfruit, in 1789. On 28 April, when Bligh and 18 members of his crew were cast adrift in an open boat, his first officer, Acting-Lieutenant Fletcher Christian and the other mutineers sailed the *Bounty* back to Tahiti. However, fearing retribution and knowing that they would be hanged if the warships of the Royal Navy ever caught up with them, the mutineers decided to seek refuge elsewhere. They knew about the discovery of Pitcairn Island by Philip Carteret aboard HMS *Swallow* some 20 years earlier and so, while 16 mutineers resolved to stay in Tahiti, nine of them led by Fletcher Christian and accompanied by 12 Tahitian women and six men sailed to Pitcairn, 1300 miles away to the south-east, and there stripped the *Bounty* and scuttled her.

By 1808, when the American ship *Topaz* called at Pitcairn in search of seals, only one of the mutineers was still alive—the others, including the ringleader, Fletcher Christian, had been killed through quarrels and fighting each other. The sole survivor, with a few Tahitian women and some of the mutineers' children, was Alexander Smith, who had changed his name to John Adams, the 'chief' of the tiny community. He had adopted the beliefs of the Seventh-day Adventists, using the *Bounty* Bible to give his people religious instruction and educate the children. When the British frigates *Briton* and *Tagus* arrived at Pitcairn in 1814 in search of the mutineers, Adams was given a full pardon and permitted to remain on the island.

When, in 1856, the population had become too large for Pitcairn's limited resources, the 194 inhabitants were, at their own request, moved to Norfolk Island, some 900 miles east of the New South Wales coast of Australia, aboard the *Morayshire*. While most of them were content to form a 'separate and distinct settlement, on picturesque Norfolk Island with its delightful climate, some families elected to return to Pitcairn in later years, and their descendants, many of them bearing the name 'Christian' and that of other mutineers, are living there today.

Summing-up. The foregoing exercise is a complete example of how stories evolve from a basic list of stamps, and how stamp pictures can be related to the characters and events described. It is apparent that, with a narrative like the mutiny on the *Bounty*, one requires a background knowledge of geographical locations and the historical sequence of events. The *Bounty* story is recorded in books on naval history (available from most public libraries), while concise biographies of Bligh, Christian and John Adams can be found in *Chambers'* and *Webster's* admirable *Biographical Dictionaries*. There are also books on Pitcairn, with useful references in the annual *Statesman's Year-Book* and the famous *Whitaker's Almanack*, both available in the libraries. And don't forget that the stamps themselves provide lots of relevant information.

Whatever your subject, there are books about it, as you will soon discover. For general information on an immense variety of subjects you should refer to the popular *Pears Cyclopedia* or the mammoth *Encyclopaedia Britannica*. Information about the countries of the world, their peoples, cities, industries and products can be found in the various year-books and travel guides to be found on library shelves, as well as biographies of composers, painters, explorers, military and naval heroes, kings and queens. You may find your special subject featured in one of the little *Observer* books published by Frederick Warne, ranging through Natural History, Sport, Transport, Architecture, Arts and Crafts, History and Travel. Subjects include Astronomy, Cats and Dogs, Wild Animals, Flags, Heraldry, Pottery and Porcelain.

It's a good idea—if you are really committed to a subject or theme—to build up your own reference library, augmented by articles from magazines and cuttings clipped from newspapers. Remember to annotate cuttings with the name of the newspaper and date. These can be filed in folders or large envelopes for easy reference. Similarly any philatelic information you might need can be obtained from stamp catalogues and magazines—indeed, the postal history of a country is one of the most popular collecting themes. The narrative would commence with the earliest postal services, illustrated by postmarks and covers, and continue with the country's first stamps, the establishment of post offices and the development of postal routes, airmails, etc. It's your choice!

ALBUMS AND WRITING-UP

The time will come when you have accumulated sufficient stamps—all arranged neatly in a 'slip-in' collecting book or one of the stock-books used by dealers—to turn your thoughts to the purchase of a suitable album and the arrangement of your stamps within it. The range of stamp albums is enormous, but your choice can be narrowed down to accommodate the type and size of collection you have embarked upon. You will require a loose-leaf album with blank leaves, and the better quality leaf will enable you to complete your writing-up or 'typing-up' without any qualms. Have a look at some albums in the dealer's shop and try to visualise your stamps arranged in them. Settle for a good, strong 'springback' binder in a colour which attracts you. If your collection is already in the hundreds, the large-format album— usually about 11 inches (deep) by 9 inches (across)—may suit you best. But for a smaller 'narrative' collection, perhaps the medium size album with leaves approximately $10\frac{1}{2} \times 8\frac{1}{2}$ inches will be most suitable.

If you want an album which lies flat when opened on a desk or table, then you will need one with double linen-hinged leaves, a multi-ring album with the appropriate leaves or one of the more expensive peg-fitting albums. The larger 'standard' size albums usually contain a 100 leaves, the smaller medium size, 50 leaves, but of course you can buy extra leaves and most binders hold a few more leaves than actually supplied. You may also want to replace some of the leaves in your album if you have spoilt a page or wish to change the arrangement of your stamps—all the leaves in the albums described are interchangeable.

Remember also that you may want a second (matching) album at some future time as your collection expands—it is wise to select one from a well-established range by one of the leading publishers to be virtually certain of being able to buy additional volumes. Some albums are supplied in protective cardboard cases and it is a good idea to keep them thus, preferably standing upright on a shelf or in a bookcase or cupboard. Stacking albums flat, one on the other, could be extremely harmful to the stamps, especially in any kind of moist, damp atmosphere. Protective transparent interleaving can be obtained for most albums.

Writing-up must not be allowed to dominate the album page. Its purpose is simply to identify the stamp pictures in a subject collection, or to provide a concise running commentary to the narrative collection. In either case the first considerations are the allocation of adequate space for both stamps and writing-up, and the planning of the arrangement and layout for each page. You will be guided by the stamps you already have, remembering to make some provision for other stamps which you know exist (from your catalogue lists), and which you will be adding to your collection as it grows and expands.

Adding stamps to the subject collection is a comparatively simple matter, whether you have just the one topic or a group of sub-divisions or different classifications. 'Flowers', for example, could be arranged in botanical families or grouped simply as 'Lilies', 'Orchids', 'Roses' or 'Tulips', etc. Just add the stamp to the next vacant space on the album page with its identifying caption. If you are writing your captions by hand, there is no problem, but of course you would be unable to add a typewritten caption unless you adopted a system of small typed labels gummed into position. If you have a neat hand, or can cultivate one with practice, the advantages are obvious.

As we have seen with the 'Bounty' story, the narrative collection can be pre-planned throughout with a synopsis of the story on the first page and each stage of it represented on the following pages, which could be headed by brief extracts, dates, etc. from the introduction with predestined spaces and captions for the stamps. Any gaps will be an incentive to acquire the stamps, although some collectors prefer not to mount and arrange a narrative

---

B L I G H   of the   B O U N T Y

William Bligh was born in Plymouth in c. 1753. He joined the Royal Navy and sailed with Captain Cook to the Pacific on the Resolution in 1772-75.

Capt. Cook
and H.M.S.
Resolution

Resolution
in 1774

In 1787 Lieutenant Bligh sailed from Portsmouth in command of H.M. Armed Vessel Bounty (formerly the Bethia) for Tahiti to collect breadfruit plants for transplantation to the West Indies.

Bounty

Fletcher
Christian
on Bounty

Breadfruit

The easy life on Tahiti demoralised Bligh's men and on the return journey the harsh discipline he imposed antagonised the crew and a mutiny led by Acting-Lieutenant Fletcher Christian took place on 28 April 1789.

Fletcher
Christian

Bligh and 18 loyal members of his crew were cast adrift in a longboat, while the mutineers returned to Tahiti. Bligh navigated the longboat westward to Timor - a voyage of some 3600 miles.

Bligh and followers
cast adrift

collection until they have virtually all the stamps they need — it all depends on the extent of the theme. If the collection is being augmented with one or two photographs, picture postcards or postmarks, these also must be acquired and accounted for in the planning stage. The best plan is to assemble all your available material and lay it out loosely on the album pages (something like an artist's 'rough'), making pencil notes, either lightly on the pages or separately, of what is going where. Ideally, prepare a rough draft of each page on separate paper. All your efforts will be rewarded when the project is completed!

26A Two pages from thematic collections—a 'Narrative' page telling part of the 'Bounty' story, and a 'Subject' page from a Literary Figures collection showing Charles Dickens.

DISPLAYS FOR EXHIBITION

Learning from others—that is the key to success in national and international competitions. Visit the next big stamp show—Autumn 'Stampex', for the Mailcoach Trophy Competition, and study other people's exhibits, particularly the award-winning ones. Note the arrangements and layouts, the methods of writing-up, and just how attractively the theme is defined and presented. Make a vow to do better! The first practical step is to obtain a copy of the Exhibition prospectus containing the rules and requirements for competition entries. These will stipulate a certain number of sheets in a specific size and of course all the conditions outlined must be adhered to.

For thematic entries marks or points are awarded for presentation and general (or 'first') impression, philatelic knowledge and condition, etc. of the stamps. Evidence of study and systematic arrangement gain more marks for the subject collection, while originality and development of the theme attract substantial marks for the narrative entry. Both types of entry must have an appropriate title and an introduction or outline plan, followed by a 'clear and concise descriptive text'. Entries must be clean and neat, and 'present a harmonious entity'. Plainly, the subject entry requires thorough research to demonstrate your knowledge of it, while the narrative must be as compact and as complete as possible. You will almost certainly be limited to nine or twelve sheets and these may have to be specially prepared—it is useless just extracting a few pages from your album, hoping thereby to impress the judges.

If you belong to a local philatelic society and you have prepared a display which you have in mind to submit to one of the national exhibitions, try and arrange a 'trial run' on club night—perhaps a society competition—and seek the opinions of your friends and fellow collectors. Some improvements may be suggested or some faults pointed out, omissions queried. Having survived the criticism (and having put matters right) you need have no qualms about entering your masterpiece in a national competition. At least your entry will be displayed and will interest other collectors. And if you don't succeed the first time (in winning a medal), remember the old proverb—try, try again!

27 Army—military uniforms (Guernsey).

28 Authors— characters from a book by Jane Austen.

29 Badges & Crests— heraldic devices make an unusual but fascinating collecting subject.

ABC OF SUBJECTS AND THEMES

Themes illustrated are shown in italics.

A   Advertising; Aeronautics; Agriculture; Aircraft; Air Forces; Airlines; Airmails; Airports; Airships and Balloons; The Alps; Americana; Animals; Antarctica; Antiques; Apiculture; Archaeology; Archery; Architecture; The Arctic; *The Army*; Artifacts; Arts and Galleries; Astronauts; Astronomy; Athletics; Atomic Installations; *Authors*; Aviation; Aztec Civilization.

B   *Badges and Crests*; Bananas; Banking; Beards; Beetles; Bells; The Bible; Bicycles; Birds; Biology; Books; Boots and Shoes; Bridges; Buddhism; *Butterflies*.

C   Calligraphy; Canals; Cats; Carpets; Cattle; Ceramics; Chess; Children; Christmas; Churches and Cathedrals; The Cinema; Coal and Mining; Cocoa; Churchill; Coffee; *Coins*; Colleges; Commercial Vehicles; Composers; Cook's Voyages; Costumes; Cotton; The Crown Jewels; Crustaceans; Cruises.

D   Dairying; *Dams*; *Dancing*; Deserts; Graphic Design; Diamonds; Disasters; Doctors; Dogs; Dolls; Drama; Drugs; Drums.

E   Earthquakes and Volcanoes; Education; *Electricity*; Elephants; *Engineering*; Engraving and Engravers; Esperanto; Ethnology; Exploration and Discovery.

33 Grimsel reservoir dam.

30 Butterflies.

31 Christmas stamps feature both religions and secular designs—Nativity scene in stained glass.

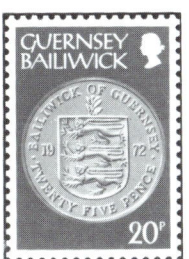

32 Guernsey 20p coin—one of a series of stamps showing coins from 1830 to the present.

34 Dancing—Cuba's National Ballet.

35 Electric light.

36 Engineering—Robert Fulton, designer of early steam ships.

F   Factories; Fairy Tales; *Famous People*; Fashion; Fencing; Firearms; Fire Services; Fishing and Fishes; *Flags*; Flowers; Flying-boats; Folklore; Food; Football; Foreign Alphabets; Forestry; Fossils; Fruits; Furniture; Furs.

G   Game (Animals, Birds, Fishes); Gardens and Fountains; *Gates and Gateways*; Gems; Geography; Geology; Girl Guides; *Glass*; Gliding; The Globe; Gold; Gothic Architecture; Grain; Greek History; Greek Mythology; Gymnastics.

38 The flag of Queen Elizabeth II as used in Australia on a stamp marking the Queen's birthday (1981).

37 Famous People—Lord Mountbatten of Burma (1900–79).

39 One of the World's most famous gateways—Paris's *Arc de Triomphe* (1806–36).

40 Stained Glass window in Freiburg Minster.

41 Heads of State—President Heinemann of West Germany (1969–74).

H Hairdressing; Handicrafts; Hands; Hats; *Heads of State*; Helicopters; Heraldry (coats of arms, etc.); Heroes and Heroines; Holiday Resorts; *Horology* (clocks and watches); Horses; Horse and Carriage; Horse-racing; Hotels; Housing; Hydro-Electric Power; Hydrology; Hymns and Hymn-writers.

I Idolatry; Inca Civilization; Insects; Insurance; Inventions and Inventors; International Organizations; *Iron and Steel*; Irrigation; Islam.

43 Iron & Steel—docks scene in India.

44 Justice—the Royal Court House in St. Peter Port, Guernsey.

42 Horology—ancient pocket watch on 1976 Europa stamp.

46 Kings and Queens—a huge field for collecting. William the Conqueror and Queen Victoria from a series depicting all British monarchs.

47 Law & Order—community policing, U.S.-style.

45 Kennedy—President Kennedy and Russian leader Nikita Khrushchev.

48 Lifeboat anniversary—a modern lifeboat from the Isle of Man.

49 Madonna—Sculpture by Ghiberti on New Zealand 1979 Christmas stamp.

J Jazz (origins); Jerusalem; The Story of Jesus; Jet Aircraft; Jewellery; Journalism; *Justice*.

K Kemal Ataturk; *President Kennedy*; Keys; Kindergarten; *Kings and Queens*.

L Labour; Lace; Lakes; Languages; *The Law*; Legends; Libraries; *Lifeboats and life-saving*; Light and lighting; Lions; Lighthouses; Literature; Lizards.

M The Mace; *Madonna*; Mail Coaches; Malaria; Mammals; Man; Manuscripts; *Maps*; Marine Life; Masks; Maya Civilisation; Medals and Decorations; Medicine; The Medical Services; Metals; Meteorology; Migration; Military Uniforms; The Moon; Monuments; Mosques; *Motherhood*; Motor Cars and Cycles; Mountains; Music.

50 Maps—a large stamp from the Falklands. Based on a map used on television news during the Falklands War.

51 Motherhood—Princess Grace of Monaco with Princess Caroline. The stamp was in fact issued to commemorate the birth of Prince Albert (1958).

52 Native life—in Togo.

53 Australian navigator—William Dampier and his ship the *Roebuck*.

54 Winter Olympics at Innsbruck.

56 Poetry—one of America's best-known poets.

55 Opera & Ballet—Danish Ballet & Music Festival, 1959—dancer in *La Sylphide*.

58 Queens—Elizabeth I on a Tristan stamp commemorating the 400th anniversary of Sir Francis Drake's circumnavigation of the World.

57 Politics—Suffragettes from the Isle of Man.

59 Radio—early equipment.

N National Anthems; *Native Life*; The Nativity; Navies of the World; *Navigation and Navigators*; Newspapers; The Nobel Prize and Winners; Novelists; Nubian Monuments; Nudes in Art; Nursing and Nurses; Nuts.

O Oil; The *Olympic Games*; *Opera and Ballet*; Optics; Orchestras and Conductors; Orchids; Organs.

P Paintings and Painters; Palaces; Parks; Parliament; Pharmaceutics; Philately; Philosophers; Photography; Physics; Physiology; Pianos; The Planets; Plants; *Poetry and Poets*; Police; *Politics and Politicians*; Ports and Harbours; Postal Services; Post Offices; Pottery; Poultry; The Press; Prisoners of War; Printing.

Q *Queens*—The Life and Times of Elizabeth I; Portraits of Queen Victoria.

R Radiation; *Radio*; Railways; *The Red Cross*; The Reformation; Refugees; Rice; Religion; The Renaissance; Reptiles; Rivers; Roads and Motorways; Road Safety;

60 Red Cross—Henri Dunant, founder.

61 Scouting—New Zealand stamp for Pan-Pacific Jamboree.

63 Toys—Teddy Bear on a Swedish Christmas stamp (1978)

67 War—Second World War American General, Douglas MacArthur.

Rockets; Roman History; Revolutions; Rotary International; Rowing; Royalty; The Royal Family; Royal Visits; Royal Weddings; Rubber; Rugby Football.

S   Sailing; Saints; Savings Banks; Schools; Science; *Scouting*; Sculpture; Seals and Charters; Seashells; Ships and Shipping; Silk-breeding; Silver; Skating; Skin-diving; Skiing; Snakes; Songs and Singers; Space Exploration; Spectacles (as worn!); Sport; Stained-glass Windows; *Stamps on Stamps*; Statesmen; Sugar; Swimming.

T   Table-tennis; Tapestries; Tea; Teaching; Telecommunications; Television; Temples; Tennis; Textiles; The Theatre; Timber; Tin; Tobacco; Tourism; Towers; *Toys*; Transport; Trees; Typography; Typewriters.

U   Uniforms; *United Nations*; U.N. Agencies; The Universe; *Universities*.

V   Vegetables; Veteran Cars; The Vatican; Victoriana; *The Vikings*; Vision.

W   *Wars*; Waterfalls; Weapons; Weaving; Whales; Wines; Winter Sports; *Famous Women*; Wonders of the World; Wood-carving; Wool; Writers.

X   *X-Rays*.

Y   *Yachts*; Youth Movements.

Z   *Zeppelins*; Zoological Gardens (and inmates).

62 Stamps on stamps—a popular theme with plenty of issues to collect.

65 Universities— a modern building at the University College of Wales, Aberystwyth. Prince Charles was a student there—another thematic link.

64 The United Nations Headquarters in New York.

70 Yachts—one of four Australian stamps featuring yachts (1981).

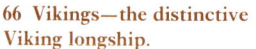

66 Vikings—the distinctive Viking longship.

68 Famous Women— concentration camp victim and diary writer Anne Frank.

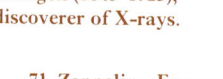

69 X-rays—Wilhelm von Röntgen (1845–1923), discoverer of X-rays.

71 Zeppelin—Europe to America flight (1930). Now a rare stamp.